ESCAPING
SPIRIT-TRAPS

POCKET EDITION

Published from
Mardukite Borsippa HQ, San Luis Valley, Colorado
Mardukite Academy & Systemology Society
for spiritual or educational purposes only

ESCAPING
SPIRIT-TRAPS

Systemology
Professional Course
Booklet #6

Developed by Joshua Free
for the Systemology Society

ISBN : 978-1-961509-30-6

Pocket Paperback Edition — *November 2023*

mardukite.com

Chart Your Flight For Ascension...
Then Let Your Spirit Fly!

Unlock your ultimate spiritual potential by removing barriers to your true native state.

Learn how to easily attain Self-actualization and help to actualize others along the way.

A greater appreciation and understanding of *Spiritual Life* and *Existence* awaits you. Expand your reach to achieve your dreams.

Each 'Professional Course' lesson-booklet offers simple exercises and techniques that directly apply the philosophy of Systemology, assisting to increase your true knowingness, improve your capabilities in this life, and even decide what you will do in your next.

At the Mardukite Academy of Systemology, the 'Professional Course' lessons in this series are presented to Seeker's that have completed the 'Basic Course', previously released as six lesson-booklets, or the six-in-one single volume edition "Fundamentals of Systemology."

This all new presentation of the Systemology 'Pathway-to-Ascension' takes Seekers and continuing students from "Zero" to "Infinity" at lightning-fast speeds!

Discover Who You Really Are...
Because You Were Never Human

<u>Fundamentals of Systemology</u>
Basic Course Lesson Booklet Series

#1 – *Being More Than Human*
#2 – *Realities In Agreement*
#3 – *Windows To Experience*
#4 – *Ancient Systemology*
#5 – *A History of Systemology*
#6 – *Systemology Processing*

<u>The Pathway to Ascension</u>
Professional Course Lesson Booklet Series

#1 – *Increasing Awareness*
#2 – *Thought & Emotion*
#3 – *Clear Communication*
#4 – *Handling Humanity*
#5 – *Free Your Spirit*
#6 – *Escaping Spirit-Traps*
#7 – *Eliminating Barriers*
#8 – *Conquest of Illusion*
#9 – *Confronting the Past*

...more titles in this series coming soon!

TABLET OF CONTENTS

COURSE INTRODUCTION

– Welcome, Seeker! . . . 11
– A New View of the Human Spirit . . . 13
– Studying the Professional Course . . . 17
– Charting a Course on the Pathway . . . 22
– Taking Flight on the Pathway . . . 25

LESSON SIX:
ESCAPING SPIRIT-TRAPS

– Being at Cause . . . 33
– Basic Processing . . . 35
– Processing "Invalidation" . . . 42
– "Hostile-Acts" and "Hold-Outs" . . . 49
– "Spirit-Traps" and "Reality" . . . 53
– Some Basic Techniques . . . 60
– Escaping the Traps . . . 64
– Reaching Further . . . 70

APPENDIX

– Glossary . . . 74
– Additional Resources . . . 89

PROFESSIONAL
COURSE
INTRODUCTION

WELCOME, SEEKER!
LET'S CHART YOUR JOURNEY
ON THE PATHWAY

Systemology is a "holistic" approach to understanding the human experience. It is not actually a singular "subject" in itself, but rather, a new way in which to view the many subjects of *Life* and all *Existence.*

This is a professional course in *Systemology*—specifically, how to *apply* the spiritual philosophy of *Mardukite Systemology* as a personal *"Pathway"* to *Ascension.* Our *Systemology* is a new approach to *"Self-Actualization."* It is completely relevant for the modern age and the future; and quite different from any previous similar attempts, or other traditions, you might find. What's more: it is applicable to anyone with any background.

This *"Professional Course"* series of lessons (booklets) immediately follows the material given in the *"Basic Course"* series — available as six separate pocket-sized booklets, or in a single hardcover volume titled: *"Fundamentals of Systemology: A New Thought For The 21st Century."*

This is a *new* presentation of *Systemology*, emphasizing the application of our philosophy for those *Seekers* that are *"Flying-Solo"* — or else working through their studies and exercises as solitary practitioners. This is a new innovation for *Systemology*. Aside from the book *"Crystal Clear,"* all of our former advanced courses have placed a focus on *"Traditional Piloting"* — where experienced practitioners assist *Seekers* in *"processing."*

To receive the greatest benefit from this study: it is expected that a *Seeker* will already be familiar with the fundamental concepts and terminology (previously relayed in the *Basic Course*) before using lessons from the *Professional Course.* This will allow us to cover the extensive territory of the *Pathway* much more quickly. However, for reference, a basic "*glossary*" of vocabulary used in this lesson is provided in the "*appendix.*"

A NEW VIEW OF THE HUMAN SPIRIT

Systemology is not a religion and does not require any type of *faith*. It is, however, built upon a "spiritual" premise—and as such is an "applied spiritual philosophy." It is based on ancient teachings that we are *Spiritual Beings* essentially "wearing" bodies like clothes—or using them as "vehicles." Yet our true native nature is not *physical,* but beyond this existence; and we can certainly operate a "body" from *outside* of it.

We are **all** *Spiritual Beings*—each of us a *unit* of *Spiritual Awareness*—that have experienced a very long *Spiritual Timeline* of existence. Although we might be particularly attached to the familiar "physical shells" associated with *this* lifetime, our true "*Spiritual Lifetime*" is seemingly *eternal*. We have been many things before *Human*, and we go onward as a *Spiritual Being* after our "*genetic vehicle*" of *this* incarnation perishes.

While a "spiritual" view of the *Human Condition* may not seem unique to our philosophy, just how often is the concept treated *systematically*? For that matter: just how many people, supposedly raised to this or that religion, or professing to believe one thing or another, actually live their lives as though they are *Spirits*?

As *Spiritual Beings* of immortal existence and infinite potential, we are not simply the "*creations*" of an even greater *Being-*

ness; we are, in fact, an integral part of that "*creative force*" which permeates all existence.

Our basic nature is to be a "*creative being*"—our highest goals are "*to create.*" And as such a being—which we refer to as an *Alpha-Spirit* in *Systemology*—we have run into some difficulties along the course of our *Spiritual Timeline* and found ourselves trapped within material *Universes* of our own collaborative *creation.*

Since we did not start out our existence in a trapped condition, it is correct to say that we have "*fallen*" from our native "*godlike*" states. It did not happen all at one, but progressively and systematically. We know our "troubles" have resulted from accumulated "barriers" and "blockages"—or *fragmentation*—during our vast experiences as *Spiritual Beings*. They are not because we lack something; but because of what's been added.

In *Systemology*, we systematically examine those routes by which we must have descended to reach our present condition, then reverse the direction of travel and chart a personal *"Pathway to Ascension."* Of course, the exact "details" of the *Spiritual Timeline* will be different for each individual *Seeker*. However, we have been able to systematically chart our *Pathway* based on common patterns of *Human fragmentation*.

In the most basic terms: the *fragmentation* that defines our "downward spiral" consists of decisions or considerations where we deny our true nature. This includes those decisions to *"withdraw"* rather than *"reach"*; where we choose to *not-know* rather than *know*; to *not-communicate* rather than *communicate*; and ultimately, to take *no-responsibility* for being a *creative-cause*, and therefore succumb to being an *effect*.

But there is *hope!* And much more importantly: there is an effectively workable *way out* of the mazes and traps of our existence. If you are reading this now, you have already begun to gather your tools and build up the *"horsepower"* necessary to break the gravity holding your *Spiritual Beingness* to the *Human Condition.*

STUDYING THE PROFESSIONAL COURSE

Most *Seekers* study and practice *Systemology* at-a-distance and independent of the "Mardukite Academy" or any "Master-level" mentors trained therein. This means that the *books* (and to a lesser degree, the *internet*) are the only means of direct contact a *Seeker* maintains with the "Systemology Society" during their studies. A continuing *Seeker* from the *"Basic Course"* will be familiar with the style of study found in *this* course.

Misunderstood words are the most common reason an individual abandons studying a subject. When a misunderstanding occurs, *Awareness* declines. These misunderstandings start to "stack up" after the first occurrence, and as a result, the level of interest and attention will also decline. This is how a "confusion" develops; and the individual will get "bored" with the subject, feel tired, and unable to concentrate.

One solution is to return to the part of the material that was still interesting and enjoyable to read. When scanning around that area of text, there is likely to be a new word (or new specific use of a familiar word) that is unclear, but was passed by unnoticed. All *Systemology* books include their own *glossary*. Using this *glossary* and a high-quality dictionary will help resolve this misunderstanding once it is located.

An effective education of any subject is taught on a *gradient*. This is what is intended by presenting the study of something as "*grades*." Rather than treating a subject as one total mass, true learning is achieved by increasing one's understanding with a *gradual* increase upward. The *ascent* to a mountaintop is not successfully achieved in one leap, but by targeting and reaching specific checkpoints along the way.

This *Professional Course* consists of a series of lessons (booklets) that gradually increase a *Seeker*'s ability to understand and apply the practices and techniques of *Systemology* as a complete "*Pathway to Ascension.*" It is an appropriate study for continuing *Seekers* (from the *Basic Course*), but also "advanced" *Systemologists*.

Each lesson (booklet) of the *Professional Course* applies *Systemology* to a particular subject (or focus). It is best if the entire course can be studied and applied in sequential order. These lessons also employ a style of practice or technique called *"Systematic Processing."* An introduction to applying this methodology is provided in the final lesson (booklet) of the *Basic Course*—or in the *"Fundamentals of Systemology"* volume.

To study the *Professional Course* just like a student at the Academy: a *Seeker* reads through all instructional material and applies each exercise (or *"process"*) presented in the text to the extent they comfortably can, before continuing on to the next lesson (booklet).

When first starting on the *Pathway* as a *Solo* practitioner, without the aid of an experienced *Pilot*, a *Seeker* shouldn't "push too hard" or allow themselves to get too "stuck" on any one area (lesson) or *process*. It is not expected that any one area will be completely handled when first introduced. For optimum results, it is expected that a serious *Seeker* will make more than one "pass" through the entire *Professional Course.*

The *Professional Course* is not altogether different from other forms of practical or technical education: where the instruction and exercises are delivered to a completion, and then a student further increases their abilities, strength and skill-level by applying additional practice throughout their life. Therefore, a student should not concern themselves with perfectly mastering each step (or lesson) before progressing forward.

Additional passes through the material are likely to result in different "*realizations*" (an increased *level of understanding*) than a previous time. New "layers" of *Knowingness* may now be accessible during a *process* that may not have been before. It is important to avoid invalidating the progress you've made just because one area is not completely handled right away, or if a certain *process* seems too difficult on the first pass.

CHARTING A COURSE ON THE PATHWAY

Although we can communicate a systematic structure to *fragmentation,* the personal journey experienced along the *Pathway* will be different for each *Seeker.* For example, certain areas will seem more *"turbulent"* or difficult for one *Seeker* than another. We tend to say that these areas have more *"charge"* on them—or that they are more *"heavily charged."* It is best to handle such areas when you are already feeling "good" and not in a situation (or condition) where that specific area is consistently being *"triggered"* or *"restimulated."*

22

As an applied philosophy, *Systemology* "theory" can be easily utilized in the "laboratory" of the "world-at-large" in everyday life. This is implied within the basic instruction of each lesson. Unlike other "sciences" that conduct experiments by making a change to some "objective variable" *out there* and waiting to see an effect, our focus is the individual (or *Observer*) themselves, and how *they* affect the "*Reality*" perceived.

In addition to applying *Systemology* "New Thought" to everyday life, our philosophy is applied by using specific exercises and systematic techniques. These "*processes*" provide the most stable personal gain (and *realizations*) for each area; but only when actually applied with a *Seeker's* full "*presence*" and *Awareness*.

This *Professional Course* is designed so that it may be easily read and studied with little concern for what "dangers" these teachings—or *processing*—might unleash. However, there are still some guidelines that pertain to the "best-uses" of these course lessons, particularly if a *Seeker* intends for stable development.

Skipping over too much material/*processing* in early lessons may make attempts to understand (or apply) later lessons more difficult. However, once the complete *Professional Course* is worked through at least once in its entirety, specific areas can then be later returned to and treated with a greater sense of *Awareness* and *"presence"* than before. Of course, in *"Traditional Piloting,"* the rate of processing is monitored by an experienced practitioner; but in *"Solo-Processing,"* a *Seeker* must regulate their own progress on the *Pathway*.

Applying a systematic technique is called *"running a process."* The *processes* are designed with very simple instructions or "*command-lines*." To *run* a *processing command-line*, a *Seeker* may be assisted by the communication of that *line* from a "*Co-Pilot*" (as in "*Traditional Piloting*"). But even then, a *Seeker* must still personally "input" the *command* as *Self*. For this reason —and quite thankfully— *Solo-Processing* is possible.

TAKING FLIGHT ON THE PATHWAY

Processing Techniques are intended to treat the *Spiritual Being* or *Alpha-Spirit*; the individual themselves. It is applied by the *Alpha-Spirit*—then *Self-directed* to the "Mind-System" or even a "body" (*genetic-vehicle*), both of which are "constructs" that the *Alpha-Spirit* (*Self*, or the "I-AM" *Awareness unit*) operates, but neither of which is actually *Self*. *Fragmentation* causes *Humans* to falsely identify *Self as* the "*Mind*" or even a "*Body*."

The *Professional Course* lessons (booklets) are designed for the *Beginning Seeker* in mind—one that may have an understanding of theory, but with little experience in practice. That being said: each of these lessons may be used toward total *Beta-Defragmentation* within a specific area. There are also more *processes* given for each subject than may be necessary to achieve an *ultimate end-point realization* on that entire area.

Some *processes* can be treated quite lightly at first; others may require a bit of working at in order to get "*running*" well. It is important to set aside a period of time when you can be dedicated to your studies and *processing*. This period of time is referred to as a "*processing session.*" The reason for this, is that when a *process* does start *running* well, it is important to be able to complete it to a satisfactory "*end-point.*"

The purpose of *systematic processing* is to be able to *really* "look" at things and even determine the *considerations* we have made—or attitudes we have decided—about *Reality* as a result of those experiences. It doesn't do us much good to simply "glance"—or to *restimulate* something uncomfortable and then quickly *withdraw* from it once again, leaving more of our *attention* yet again behind and held fixedly on it.

Generally speaking, a *Seeker* continues to *run* a *process* so long as something is "happening"—which is to say, the *process* is still producing a change. Usually this is evident by the type of "answers" that a *command-line* helps a *Seeker* originate from the database of their own *Mind-System*. The *command-lines* do not "do" anything on their own. They assist a *Seeker* to direct their own attention toward increasing *Awareness*.

Of course, a *Seeker* may also cease to generate new "data" from a *process* without reaching an *"ultimate" realization* as an *"end-point."* It is possible that additional "layers" (or even other "areas") require handling before anything "deeper" is accessible. If this is the case, end the *process.* But, if a *Seeker* is *withdrawing* from something uncomfortable that was incited or stirred up, then a *process* is *run* until they feel "good" about it.

In case the thought of encountering *"turbulence"* is a concern: the techniques given as *"Opening Procedures"* of a *Formal Session* (in the *Basic Course*), and those found in the earliest lessons of the *Professional Course*, are quite useful when applied as "safety nets" for maintaining *Awareness* and *presence*, even when *Flying-Solo*.

One of the benefits to *Flying-Solo* is that *processing* is entirely *Self-determined.* This

28

already provides a certain built-in "safety" for a practitioner. Anything you *restimulate* by *Self-determinism* is *your thing.* It is not incited by external *other-determined* influences (or other "source-points" in existence) that make you an *effect*. It can be more easily handled in *processing* — or you can simply let things "cool down" and come back to it again.

While it may seem "mysterious" to beginners, a *Seeker* gets a sense for knowing how long to *run* a *process* only with practice. Once you have spent some time actually applying the *Professional Course*, there are many aspects that become "second nature" because they are, in fact, a part of our true original nature. All we have done is *"reverse engineer"* the routes of *creation* and *consideration* that are already *our own.*

LESSON SIX:
ESCAPING
SPIRIT TRAPS

BEING AT CAUSE

In our previous lesson (booklet)—"*Free Your Spirit*"—we began to explore the true nature of the *Alpha-Spirit*, or the *actual Self*, as a *Spiritual Awareness* capable of experiencing existence from any *viewpoint*. That we seem to have fixed our *attention* and total *consideration* of our own *Beingness* solely as the "*Human Condition*" is unfortunate. But, it does not have to be permanent.

Early on our *Spiritual Timeline*—or our sense of personal "history" as an *Alpha-Spirit* (that we often refer to as the "*Backtrack*")—we are *knowingly* acting as an "*Eternal Being*" with seemingly infinite creative abilities. This is when we were the *most* at "*Cause*" over our own *Beingness*, our *creations*, and our experience of *existence*.

Of course, being at *Cause* means also *doing* or *creating* things that one may later regret. This starts a chain of *inhibition* toward future *action* and *creation*. By experiencing *guilt* or *shame*, an individual may even begin to *hold-back* their *communication* with others. Accumulated *fragmentation* like this in specific areas led to an *Alpha-Spirit* restricting its own *active abilities* and *willingness* to *reach*—increasingly *withdrawing*, as *Cause*.

In *Systemology Level-2*, our *systematic processing* emphasis is on *"doing things"*—which is to say, the *things we have done*. It is only after the area of *"doing things"* is *confronted* easily, that we systematically consider additional matters of *ethics*, *justification* and *responsibility*.

When this subject is initially raised, the first things you might think of concern only the most serious crimes and conceptions of *"evil."* But that is only one small part of our *spiritual rehabilitation*.

The truth is that once we begin to *hold-back* or *inhibit* certain areas (or *channels*) reactively or on automatic, we stop *knowingly* being at *Cause* for that entire area — and we may even miss out on experiencing the "good things" there too.

BASIC PROCESSING

We begin this lesson by digging right in: peeling back layers of what we may easily *recall* and *consider*, much as we did for the general area of *"communication"* in earlier lessons (booklets). The goal is to again *"break through"* various *barriers* of *fragmentation* that inhibits a *Seeker's* free *consideration* and *willingness*.

In later *processing levels*, we are more concerned with what an individual considers they *"should"* or *"shouldn't"* do — or else, what you ultimately decide *to do* in the future. But before this may be experienced in *Self-honesty*, the *fragmented inhibition* that underlies free *consideration* about *action* must be handled (or rather, *defragmented*).

For *systematic processing*: we are concerned with "*spotting*" (*identifying* and *noticing* something about) a particular *action*, and then observing if there is any particular "*resistance*" to thinking about it, or any emotional "*turbulence*" attached to *considerations* of that *action*.

On a higher-level of application, the *Pathway-to-Ascension* is a progressive "*rehabilitation*" of the native or original *spiritual ability* of the individual (*Seeker*, &tc.) who IS the "*Alpha-Spirit*" themselves. But being wrapped up in many layers and lifetimes worth of *restrictive fragmentation* inhibits true *Knowingness* of that state.

When this *Level* of *processing* is first introduced in *Traditional Piloting*, the *Seeker* is not required to give a verbal "answer" to a specific *"processing command-line"* (or "PCL") if they are uncomfortable in doing so. In this case, they simply acknowledge that they have *considered* an *answer*.

In *Systemology Level-2*, a *Seeker* may benefit from starting off *Flying-Solo*, and then *processing* any remaining *turbulent fragmentation* with *Traditional Piloting*. As usual, we will start off with light *processes* to open up the areas we will handle throughout this lesson.

Each PCL series (below) is cycled through multiple times as a complete *process*. To *run* these most effectively, a continuing *Seeker/student* should apply what they have learned about *systematic processing* in earlier lessons that included similarly-styled *processes*.

Willingness to Do
 1. *"What would you be willing to do?"*

2. *"What would you be willing to have someone do?"*

3. *"What would you be willing to have others do?"*

Willingness to Reveal

1. *"What would you be willing to reveal?"*

2. *"What would you be willing to have someone reveal?"*

3. *"What would you be willing to have others reveal?"*

A *Seeker* may *run* the following process *Solo*, recording the data on paper (to see it "external" from *Self*), but then destroying (burning) it afterward. This allows a *Seeker* to *run* it without "worrying someone will find out" (which, itself, is another matter taken up later on).

A. *"What shouldn't others know about you?"*

B. *"Who would it be safe to communicate that to?"*

C. *"What shouldn't someone know about others?"*

D. *"Who would it be safe to communicate that to?"*

Once this area has been approached as a general area, *processing* may then be directly applied to various *"terminals"* ("persons," "places," "things," &tc). As a standard, we start by *processing* basic *terminals* that represent each of the *"Spheres of Existence"* (introduced in *Lesson 2* of the *"Basic Course"*). These include: "YOUR BODY"; "A FAMILY MEMBER"; "CHILDREN"; "SEX"; "WORK"; "SOCIETY"; "LIFE ON EARTH"; "PHYSICAL MATTER"; and "THOUGHT" (or "SPIRITS"). On additional (advanced) passes through this course material later on, consider also "CREATION" and "DESTRUCTION."

The *"terminals"* (given above) are general examples. Other similar (but more specific) *terminals* with *turbulent fragmentation* may be used in place of them. For example: "A HUSBAND" (for "Family Member"), "HOUSEKEEPING" (for "Work"), or "AN AUTOMOBILE" (for "Physical Matter").

This *processing formula* includes several individual *processes* that are used together to form a complete *routine* for *running* a particular *terminal* in this area of "*doing things*." A *routine* such as this is preferably handled within a single *session*. Insert the "terminal name" into the following *formula*:

A1. "*What have you done involving ---?*"

A2. "*What have you held-back from doing involving ---?*"

B1. "*What has someone else, or others, done involving ---?*"

B2. "*What has someone else, or others, held-back from doing involving ---?*"

C1. "*What would you permit someone, or others, to do involving ---?*"

C2. *"What have you kept someone else, or others, from doing involving ---?"*

D1. *"What could you permit others to find out about you involving ---?"*

D2. *"What have you held-out from communicating about ---?"*

E1. *"What could someone, or others, let you find out about themselves involving ---?"*

E2. *"What have others held-out from communicating about ---?"*

The "ultimate" *process* for this area is *run* after *all* previous *processing* given in this section. It does not apply "terminals"; it assists with stabilizing results and/or prompting *end-point realizations* for this level of *processing* as a whole.

A1. *"What have you done?"*

A2. *"What have you held-back from doing?"*

B1. *"What has someone else (or others) done?"*

B2. *"What has someone else (or others) held-back from doing?"*

C1. *"What would you permit someone (or others) to do?"*

C2. *"What have you kept someone (or others) from doing?"*

D1. *"What could you permit someone (or others) to find out about you?"*

D2. *"What have you held-out from communicating?"*

E1. *"What could someone (or others) let you find out about them?"*

E2. *"What have others held-out from communicating?"*

PROCESSING "INVALIDATION"

Ultimately, at the basic core of the matter, *abilities* of an *Alpha-Spirit* can only be weakened or "lost" by their own decision. These kind of decisions are sometimes known as *"postulates"* or *Alpha-Thought*. They are the *Alpha-Spirit's* prime decision for something *"to be"* or *"not-be"* what it *Is*. This includes an individual's own *Beingness*, their own "sense" of *Self*—and decisions about what *"Self"* ultimately *Is*.

Although the *actual decision* rests with *Self*, there are many ways in which an *Alpha-Spirit* might be influenced to make such decisions. In order for *Self* to *Be* "less" than what *Self* actually is (in its true native state), it must, by definition, be *"invalidated."*

The originating trigger or restimulation of *"invalidation fragmentation"* is usually from someone else, or others. It is only when these criticisms or opinions are, for whatever reason, actually *agreed* to as *reality* (made "one's own") from a higher-level of thought (or *postulate*) that they will affect *Self* (the *Alpha-Spirit*).

This *fragmentation* prompts an individual to start *validating* the *invalidation* and therefore make it "true" for their experience of existence (or *reality*). In common terms: it becomes a *"self-fulfilling prophecy"* of sorts. The individual now *fully* *"believes"* themselves *to be* "incapable" of an *ability*, and so essentially becomes so.

The proper way to develop, enhance, or regain, an ability, requires *validating* one's own successes—even when they are only small gains. Eventually, we want to be able to withstand *invalidation* from other outside sources as well; to *confront* their existence without *agreeing* to them ourselves. An *actualized* individual could face all the criticism in the world and be unaffected so long as they do not consider *Self* as *"less."*

A professional may make many mistakes, but the skill level increases when these are not used to *invalidate* the many accomplishments that have taken place along the way. A professional in sports continues their improvement by *validating* the many goals, hits, or scores, they have made in their career. They do not *invalidate* themselves just because of a critical miss—in spite of the "boos" and ridicule from others.

In a state of *fragmentation*—outside *Self-Honesty*—the *Human Condition* maintains a quite "fragile" sense of *Self-worth* and *certainty*. The less *actualized* an individual is, the more easily their thought processes and actions may become "unbalanced"; the more easily they may be led to *invalidate* whatever slight confidence they have. Our goal is not to run from or avoid *invalidation*, but to emphasize *validation* of the "good."

On our long journey down the *Backtrack* of existence, we have experienced a great many things on *both* sides of this area— and hence our *processing* must treat *considerations* derived from *both* sides: because we have all participated in *invalidating* each other at some point or another. This even led us to being more susceptible to its *effects*, ourselves.

One reason we do not want to act in "avoidance" of *invalidation*, is because operating in such a manner often includes *"holding-back"* as a mechanism. To avoid any possibility of *invalidation*, or situations where one may encounter it, the individual holds themselves back from reaching into entire areas of existence.

The following two basic *processes* are *run* to explore *considerations* on the subject of *invalidation*.

A1. *"How could you avoid invalidation?"*

A2. *"How could you attract invalidation?"*

B1. *"How could someone else (or others) avoid invalidation?"*

B2. *"How could someone else (or others) attract invalidation?"*

This next *process* applies *"analytical recall"* to the *"circuits."*

1. *"Recall invalidating someone."*

2. *"Recall being invalidated."*

3A. *"Recall someone else invalidating another (or others)."*

3B. *"Recall someone else invalidating themselves."*

0. *"Recall invalidating yourself."*

Now we apply a combination of traditional *"New Thought"* and *Systemology* to start handling specifics. The first PCL is:

A. *"What might you be invalidated for?"*

Once the *Seeker* has an "answer" that may be *processed*, the following two PCL are *run* until some sense of "relief" or "release" is experienced. Then use the first PCL (above) to locate and *run* another *invalidation*. *"Invalidation"* means "making less of." In this *process*, we are focusing on *imagining* the "opposite" of *invalidation* taking place: *validating* an individual's true *Spiritual Beingness* as they are (or appear to be).

B. *"Imagine someone else validating you for having it."*

C. *"Imagine someone else having a similar disability or weakness; then imagine yourself validating them for having it."*

Running processes for the conceptual areas of *"criticism"* and *"judgment"* is closely related to *"invalidation."* Therefore, consider tolerable *"acceptance"* and *"rejection"* for *all three areas.* These may be run consecutively (one after another, each concept applied as its own *process*). Use the concepts of "INVALIDATION"; "CRITICISM"; and "JUDGMENT" to complete the PCL below. [This "acceptance/rejection" style of *systematic processing* is introduced in *Lesson-4* of this series.]

A. *"What --- could you accept?"*

B. *"What --- could you reject?"*

"HOSTILE-ACTS" & "HOLD-OUTS"

An entire volume of the *Systemology Core*, titled *"Way of the Wizard,"* is dedicated to the subject of *"ethics."* In this present *Professional Course* series, we simplify the subject and emphasize only what directly pertains to *processing.* It is necessary for completing *"Systemology Level-2."* It is not, however, an area that many *Seekers* particularly enjoy—and thus we begin to see some of them fall by the wayside of the *Pathway* around this point of progression.

The development and use of our *Systemology* is possible so late in the *"game"* of our *Spiritual Existence*, because we have only now been able and willing to fully *observe* and *understand* the patterns of our *thoughts, behaviors,* and ultimately the *roles* that we play out, in each consecutive experience of a lifetime. Some of what we have experienced is difficult to "face"—difficult to *confront "As-It-Is"*—and yet, without doing so, we restrict ourselves from having total access to our own *Cosmic History.*

In actual truth, as *Spiritual Beings*, we have been involved in *games* of "conflict" and "domination" for a very long time. We have experienced, again, *both sides* of most everything by this point in our existence—even if we have *blocked-out* or *blacked-out* much of this memory. But memory exists in "sequences" and "chains"—and our unwillingness to *confront* something, *blocks-out* entire areas of *Knowingness* and *ability.*

We take a systematic approach to considering the mechanisms that are attached to committing a *Harmful-Act*, which is to say, an action that directly harms *someone* else—or some other *"Sphere of Existence."* This is an important area to *process* prior to any higher-level *considerations* of *"eth-ics"* or *"moral justification."*

A *Hostile-Act* or *Harmful-Act* is the start of a systematic sequence that generally results in *fragmentation.* First, there is the "act" or "action" itself. Then, the mind naturally considers *"motivation"* for that action and others similar to it. For example: when one is struck by another, there is a tendency to want to *"balance"* that action, and one *considers* that they have a *"motivation"* to strike back.

To extend this example: an individual is likely to claim that the "harm" *they have done* is *"motivated"* by the "harm" *done to them.* The *Alpha-Spirit* begins to *"postulate"* this as *reality*; the Mind-System follows by correcting its *perceptions* accordingly. But, by this insistence on manifesting a "balance" of "harm" we find the individual getting entangled in a *Spirit-Trap* that it didn't see coming.

51

Some traditions recognize a *karma*-like mechanism at play in the Universe. In most cases, however, this is usually considered as something mediated by an "outside" or "other-determined" source. The actual fact is that we impose this *karma* upon our own *reality*. And it systematically plays out like this:

Our insistence that harm "must be" balanced then leaves us with our own "unmotivated" *Harmful-Acts* that "must be" balanced by *future* "motivators." This means receiving harm in the *future* that one feels they, themselves, deserve (to balance what they have done). What's more: having committed a *Harmful-Act,* the individual starts to *"hold-out"* (*withdraw*) their communication with various individuals, groups, or even entire areas of existence.

This whole "systematic" sequence may be taking place quite *unknowingly*, because the original *"postulate"* for such automated-mechanisms to exist were put into "play" by *Self* as a *reality-agreement* long ago. But before we begin *processing* these areas, let us consider how an individual gets entangled in such *Spirit-Traps* in the first place.

"SPIRIT-TRAPS" AND "REALITY"

The subjects of *"Reality"* and *"Existence"* are approached somewhat indirectly all along the *Pathway-to-Ascension*. Our understanding of what *Is*, and the nature of our own participation with *Reality*, improves cumulatively the whole way.

Participation in this *Shared Universe* is quite similar to our experiences of the many that preceded it. This *Reality* is a "shared illusion" *created* by the *Alpha-Spirit*—the individual themselves—that is experiencing it. This is always the case, even before an *Alpha-Spirit* "shared" their *created illusions* with others, and simply *created* in isolation for one's own *Self* as a personal "Home Universe."

Although the *Alpha-Spirit* is the ultimate *creator* of their own *Reality*, there is a separation or fragmentation inherent from the beginning in order to experience that *created reality* or "illusion." Without this separation, an individual would have "total identification" with their *creation*; and in a *Shared Universe*, it would result in a "total identification" with everyone else. There would be no sense of "individuality"; there would also be no continuation of a "growth-pattern" left unattended.

Communication is an underlying factor in establishing and maintaining *reality-agreements* concerning a *Shared Universe*. To maintain "individuality" we must see the whole as a system fragmented into parts, which may then communicate with each other across a perceived distance. The continuous experience of any *Reality* (or *Universe*) is maintained by the continuous communication among those *sharing* it.

In the most material sense, *communication* is a motion, action, or relay, of a particle (or data) from a *source-point* to a *receipt-point*, across some distance of space. It is such motion that gives us a sense of "*sequential time,*" but that is not our present concern. What we are concerned with is the fact that a communication means, in essence, *duplicating* or *copying* something at a *receipt-point* the same as it exists at the *source-point*.

What we consider "*Existence*" or a *Universe* is really the continuous communication of *reality-agreements* among all those concerned. Each individual is essentially *creating* and *duplicating* the communication from their own *viewpoint*, within their own *Personal Universe*. The level or degree of actual *duplication* is reflected in the level or degree of "synchronous exchange" (or "sameness") experienced by all those sharing it.

In previous lessons, we have treated "communication" as spoken messages; but it is also reflected in the "actions" one takes with others and their environment. Actions *are* communications. They involve a relay of intention; and they are governed by the same element of *willingness* that affects our *reach* and *withdraw* in other areas of life, and in other forms of communication.

Duplication is a critical component of a *Shared Universe*. In terms of communicated action: let us consider that whether you "hug" or "harm" an individual, at some level, there is a *"mental image"* of that *reality* (and a *duplication* of it) communicated and shared between all parties (or *"terminals"*) involved.

What we essentially mean here is that: in a *Shared Universe* (or *Reality*), an individual *Alpha-Spirit* is still *creating* from within their own *Personal Universe*. However, those *creations* now include a *duplication* of shared experiences. Both the *source*-role and *effect*-role are *created* as a *reality* within the *Personal Universe* of each individual *sharing* the interaction (or communication).

In light of this, a *Seeker* may better understand why there is an emphasis on "circuits" in *systematic processing*. We are *creating*—albeit *duplicating*—and *recording data* for *all* interacting *viewpoints* (*Personal Universes* of other *Spiritual Beings*) of a shared experience as part of our own *reality* (our own *Personal Universe*).

An *Alpha-Spirit* is already experiencing some degree of *fragmentation knowingly* by engaging in a *Shared Universe*. This is what allows for a simultaneous "*individual*" and "*shared*" experience. The *duplicat-*

57

ion factor allows one to get a sense of, or feel, *both* sides of a communication—and even to *duplicate* the "opposite" role. This only works out for our benefit when interactions are those that are desirable to *both* parties.

We are in constant interaction—or communication—with others and our environment every day of our earthly lives. *Imprinting* from all of these interactions is not necessarily *persistently* and *compulsively created* as part of our more permanent *reality-agreements*, and therefore may not all be a significant source of *spiritual fragmentation*. The primary factor on this is what we are *knowingly willing* to *confront* and *accept*.

"Do unto others..." has existed as a *"Golden Rule"* for thousands of years, but failed to perfect the *Human Condition*. We are interested in the entire experience from someone else's *viewpoint*, in addition to the actions themselves. It is not a matter of whether you would like it or *accept* it from your own *viewpoint*, but whether you would like (or *accept*) it from the *viewpoint* of the *effect*-role (the "other person"), meaning *them* (as the individual *they* are).

The real *fragmentation* begins to accumulate (and *Awareness* is increasingly entangled) when an individual becomes *unwilling* to experience the *effect* they have *created*—meaning, of course, *unwilling* to *confront* the *viewpoint* of the opposing-role. Keep in mind that we are, again, referring to something that an individual is *unwilling* to *confront* and experience, that they themselves are *creating* (or *duplicating*) as *reality* for their own *Personal Universe*. And therein lies the rudiments of a *trap* for the *Awareness* of an *Alpha-Spirit*.

SOME BASIC TECHNIQUES

To start off lightly in the areas we have been discussing, alternate the following PCL:

A. *"Recall a time that was pleasant for both you and someone else."*

B. *"Imagine the experience from their viewpoint."*

Using the above *process* as an example, place an emphasis (for "Step-B") on "getting a sense of" or "feeling" things from other people's *viewpoints*. This may also be practiced as an *"objective process"* when engaging in pleasant social interactions. The goal is to *"imagine"* or *"duplicate"* the senses or impressions perceived from another *viewpoint*. For example: how *you* might look or sound to *someone else* as you talk to them.

When we speak of *Harmful-Acts*, we mean when someone else was harmed. It does not matter what the circumstances for it are—whether intentional or accidental, whether in *Self-defense* or even to protect others; if you are *unwilling* to *confront* the action, an experience of its *effects* may be waiting in your future.

In *systematic processing*, such *effects* may be "*run out*" (or "*processed out*") so that an individual is no longer *unknowingly* and *continuously* maintaining that *fragmentation* on their ongoing "*life-track.*" The most basic solution is simply to *knowingly confront* things in *processing* by using *imagined* representations.

Much of this "*karmic*" *fragmentation* lies dormant for long periods of time, which is why we seldom will experience any instantaneous "repercussion" of our actions. The "balancing" *effects* generally manifest at times and in ways that are quite far and removed from the original *imprinting incident*. As a result, this "mechanism" is not even an effective "learning tool" to properly steer an individual to a higher ethics.

As we begin to *process* more specific or direct examples, it is best to start with lighter experiences. In this case, we want to locate (or "spot") a specific instance in memory where you caused someone else harm. It does not have to be a particularly significant *Harmful-Act* at first, but should be something which you later regretted—such as "hurting someone else's feelings," &tc.

The most basic method of *confronting* the action is to *imagine* the experience from the other person's *viewpoint*; and getting a sense for how they felt at the time. In order to achieve any kind of "release" or "relief" from this exercise, you may need to alternate between the *viewpoints*: first spotting your actions from your own *viewpoint*, then spotting the event and sensations experienced from the other *viewpoint*.

If this *process* makes things seem more "heavy" or "solid"—as opposed to a sense of "relief"—then it is likely that any *turbulence* or *fragmentation* is tied strongly to a similar type of incident that happened prior to it. If this earlier incident can be located, then the same *process* (above) is applied to *that* action or event.

In the case of a *Harmful-Act* where the "victim" was not present (such as "vandalism," &tc.), a *Seeker* would *"imagine"* the scenario (and "feelings") that the other person *might* have experienced upon its discovery. Progressively work your way through whatever is easily recalled for this first pass through the materials.

While we have emphasized "out-flow" (Circuit-1) of the *Harmful-Act* itself, remember that *all viewpoints* are *duplicated* from an *imprinting incident*. This means that a "victim" may also "pull in" (Circuit-2) *fragmentation* of the opposing-role (and its "karma") as their own *reality*, by also not *confronting* it *"As-It-Is."* This is what causes individuals to *"dramatize"* (or "act out to others") what has been *done to* them.

The same techniques (previously described) are applied, but this time *running* the *processes* by *imagining* the "attackers" *viewpoint* as they commit the *Harmful-Act.* This sometimes stirs up more *emotional turbulence* than when treating one's own actions (Circuit-1). In this case, a "relief" or "release" point occurs when a *Seeker* can easily *confront* the action without any particular *compulsive* desire to do it themselves.

ESCAPING THE TRAPS

It is important to note that these *"karmic"*

mechanisms that we speak of are *not* the *only* reason that things happen. Just because someone acts against you does not mean you automatically deserved it as some kind of long-running tab of retribution. And while all "actions" have a certain *cause* and *sequence* behind them, everything that happens is *not* you pulling some cosmic destiny in on your reality. Things can *just* happen.

However, if there *is* a particularly *turbulent* area that persists in spite of your basic efforts (as given in the previous sections) to *confront* it *"As-It-Is,"* then this "trap-type" of *fragmentation* may indeed be (at least partly) *"in play."*

When *processing* these areas—particularly when *Flying-Solo*—it is preferred to focus on the *out-flows* (Circuit-1) regarding what *you have done*, because the greatest gains are achieved when *processing* toward *"being* at *cause."* Of course, a *Seeker* must also *confront in-flows* or what has been *done to them* (Circuit-2); but *running* this too long (without an alternation with *out-flows*) will tend to overemphasize *"being at effect."*

The goal of *Systemology Level-2* (in combination with *processing* from previous *levels*) is for a *Seeker* to release themselves from the heavier "energetic burdens" that they carry as a *Spiritual Being*—that which is most accessible to *process* at this stage of the *Pathway*. We mean, of course, the "unraveling" or "dissolving" of *energetic-masses* that entangle an individual's *Spiritual Awareness* into the fixed solidity of *fragmentation*.

"Withholding" things is one way our *Awareness* becomes entangled and unavailable to us. By this, we don't necessarily mean simply not saying or doing something; but when *attention* must be actively applied in order to *restrain* one's *Self* from such, then we are *"holding-back"* our *Self (unknowingly)* in other ways too.

A *"hold-back"* on action and ability generally begins with a *"hold-out"* on communication. An example of this might be to *"hold-out"* on one's true opinion of something in order to spare someone else's feelings. Another might be to *"hold-out"* sharing something that would be socially inappropriate or unacceptable. Finally, and most critically, there is what we *"hold-out"* communicating out of guilt or fear of punishment.

In a *Shared Universe*, all of these are examples where an individual goes *"out-of-communication"* with other *"terminals"* and *"Spheres of Existence."* As demonstrated throughout the previous lessons of this *Professional Course* series, this is the first factor that leads to increased *fragmentation* and various difficulties maintaining true *Self-determinism* and a *Self-Honest* experience of existence.

As an exercise in *processing out-flow*, the standard practice in *Mardukite Zuism* and the *Systemology Society* is for a *Seeker* to write "confessional letters" (while alone) —to see the events as separate from *Self* —and then immediately burn them. The practice of "confessing to another" (in *Traditional Piloting*) *does* have spiritual value, but it can also be easily abused or mishandled (and is not covered in this present lesson).

If the "confessional letter" does not provide a sense of "relief" or "release" with a particular incident, terminal or area, there is another factor that may be involved.

The *turbulence* attached to various *Harmful-Acts* increases with the amount of *attention* that an individual places on it "internally" to "keep it in check" (so to speak). This is most critical with those things we worry about *"someone finding out."* A lot of *Awareness* is suspended or fixated on *those* things—and that intense "internalization" of our *attention-energy* also has a tendency to "pull-in" a lot of what we "don't want" in our lives.

One of the reasons this area is so critical is that: similar to how the *fragmentation* of an *"imprint"* might be restimulated by a certain *"facet"* in our environment, the *energetic-turbulence* associated with a *Harmful-Act* may be stirred up reactively (automatically) when someone *almost* discovers one of our *"hold-outs."*

This "fear of discovery" causes *attention* to "invigorate" or "validate" that area again with more of our *Awareness*. And this is generally instigated or caused by an "outside" *other-determined* source. The solution is to *confront* the thing *"As-It-Is"* with high-powered *Awareness* in *processing* on one's own determination, rather than *withdrawing* from it and feeding it with low-level *attention* each time it gets restimulated.

We address this now at our present grad-

ient of the *Pathway* because: should anything similar to what we are describing
get restimulated in any *processing*, it must
be handled (with *processing*) before any
stable gains or further progress is possible. The simple fact that some "thing"
suddenly appears in *processing* generally
means it is a source of *fragmentation* that
requires getting under one's own *Self*-
control.

REACHING FURTHER

This lesson marks the completion of *Systemology Level-2*. This is a critical check-
point on the *Pathway* for *Seekers*. This is
also a point where a *Seeker* might cycle
back to the beginning of these *Professional
Course* lessons and *process* their way
through a second pass of all the materials
presented up until now.

Although the written materials (for this

level) may end here, the point to which a *Seeker* can reach with the existing *processing* given may not have been attained with their first pass.

Ideally, a *Seeker* that has fully completed *Systemology Level-2* will have a much greater and more stable certainty on "*Being* an *Alpha-Spirit* that is *having* a *Human* experience." This certainty should be at such a level as to prevent a *Seeker* from being so easily "trapped" in the "problems" of the *Human Condition* ever again.

By this, we do not mean that a *Seeker* will have completely "broken free" of the *Human Condition* at this juncture of the *Pathway.* They are still likely to experience some emotional fluctuation with daily life. But, they are not likely to become so deeply entangled in it; they have a better understanding of how the *Human "game"* is played in this world—and how to handle it well enough to continue their progress on the *Pathway.*

The final exercise given for this *processing level* should assist with these goals. It covertly emphasizes that you—as an *Alpha-Spirit*—are not *actually* "located" *anywhere*. It is simply part of our *"game"* in this existence—to *pretend* to "be" in the "locations" from which we *perceive* or *operate*.

The PCL for this exercise is:

"Close your eyes; spot places where you are not. Spot many places."

We say that our goal is "covertly" embedded in the PCL, because by "checking" that you are "not" somewhere, you tend to put *attention* on it to *look* at it—thereby transferring (or "projecting" if you prefer) some degree of personal *Awareness* to that location (which is "*exterior*" from the "*body*").

The PCL does not limit *where* these "places" are. They are "spotted" by *atten-*

tion with eyes closed; they do not need to be considered relatively "nearby." This practice is repeated until some sense of *exterior "ZU-Vision"* is achieved. At this *processing level*, these perceptions do not have to be very vivid or accurate, so long as a *Seeker* feels they have achieved an "improved" or "increased" sense of this spiritual ability.

The Systemology Professional Course
continues in the next lesson booklet:
ELIMINATING BARRIERS

GLOSSARY

actualization : to make actual, not just potential; to bring into full solid Reality; to realize fully in *Awareness* as a "thing."

agreement (reality) : unanimity of opinion of what is "thought" to be known; an accepted arrangement of how things are; things we consider as "real" or as an "is" of "reality"; a consensus of what is real as made by standard-issue (common) participants; what an individual contributes to or accepts as "real"; in *Systemology*, a synonym for "*reality.*"

alpha : the first, primary, basic, superior or beginning of some form; in *Systemology*, referring to the state of existence operating on spiritual archetypes and postulates, will and intention "exterior" to the low-level condensation and solidarity of energy and matter as the 'physical universe' (*beta*).

alpha-spirit : a "spiritual" *Life*-form; the "true" *Self* or I-AM; the *individual*; the spiritual (*alpha*) *Self* that is animating the (*beta*) physical body or "*genetic vehicle*" using a continuous *Lifeline* of spiritual ("*ZU*") energy; an individual spiritual (*alpha*) entity possessing no physical mass or measurable waveform (motion) in the Physical Universe as itself, so it animates the (*beta*) physical body or "*genetic vehicle*" as a catalyst to experience *Self*-determined causality in effect within the *Physical Universe*; a singular unit or point of *Spiritual Awareness* that is *Aware* that it is *Aware.*

alpha thought : the highest spiritual *Self-determination* over creation and existence exercised by an Alpha-Spirit; the Alpha range of pure *Creative Ability* based on direct postulates and considerations of *Beingness*; spiritual qualities comparable to "thought" but originating in Alpha-existence, independently superior to a Mind-System.

ascension : actualized *Awareness* elevated to the point of true "spiritual existence" exterior to *beta existence*. An "Ascended Master" is one who has returned to an incarnation on Earth as an inherently *Enlightened One*, demonstrable in their words and actions; they have the ability to *Self-direct* the "Mind" and "Body" as *Self* (as a "Spirit"); and to maintain consciousness as a personal identity continuum with the same *Self-directed* control and communication of Will-Intention that is exercised, actualized and developed deliberately during one's present incarnation.

associative knowledge : significance or meaning of a facet or aspect assigned to (or considered to have) a direct relationship with
another facet; to connect or relate ideas or facets
of existence with one another; in traditional systems logic, an equivalency of significance or
meaning between facets or sets that are grouped
together, such as in *(a + b) + c = a + (b + c)*; in
Systemology, erroneous associative knowledge
is assignment of the same value to all facets or
parts considered as related (even when they are
not actually so), such as in *a = a, b = a, c = a*
and so forth without distinction.

attention : active use of *Awareness* toward a
specific aspect or thing; the act of "attending"
with the presence of *Self*; a direction of focus or
concentration of *Awareness* along a particular
channel or conduit or toward a particular terminal node or communication termination
point; the Self-directed concentration of personal energy as a combination of observation,
thought-waves and consideration; focused application of *Self-Directed Awareness*.

awareness : the highest sense of-and-as *Self* in
knowing and being as I-AM (the *Alpha-Spirit*);
the extent of beingness directed as a viewpoint
(POV) experienced by *Self* as *Knowingness*.

beta (existence) : all manifestation in the "Physical Universe" (KI, in *Zuism*); the conditions of *Awareness* for the *Alpha-spirit* (*Self*) as a physical organic *Lifeform* or "*genetic vehicle*" in which it experiences causality in the *Physical Universe.*

charge : to fill or furnish with a quality; to supply with energy; to lay a command upon; in *Systemology*—to imbue with intention; to overspread with emotion; personal energy stores and significances entwined as fragmentation in mental images, reactive-response encoding and intellectual (and/or) programmed beliefs.

circuit : a circular path or loop; a closed-path within a system that allows a flow; a pattern or action or wave movement that follows a specific route or potential path only; in *Systemology*, "*communication processing*" pertaining to a specific *flow* of energy or information along a channel; "*feedback loop.*"

communication : successful transmission of information, data, energy (&tc.) along a message line, with a reception of feedback; an energetic flow of intention to cause an effect (or duplication) at a distance; the personal energy moved or acted upon by will or else 'selective directed attention'; the 'messenger action' used to transmit and receive energy across a medium; also relay of energy, a message or signal—or even locating a personal POV (viewpoint) for the Self—along the *ZU-line*.

confront : to come around in front of; to be in the presence of; to stand in front of, or in the face of; to meet "face-to-face" or "face-up-to"; additionally, in *Systemology*, to fully tolerate or acceptably withstand an encounter with a particular manifestation without an automatic reactive response..

consideration : careful analytical reflection of all aspects; deliberation; determining the significance of a "thing" in relation to similarity or dissimilarity to other "things"; evaluation of facts and importance of certain facts; thorough examination of all aspects related to, or important for, making a decision; the analysis of consequences and estimation of significance when making decisions; also in *Systemology*, the *postulate* or *Alpha-Thought* that defines the state of *beingness* for what something "*is.*"

defragmentation : the *reparation* of wholeness; collecting all dispersed parts to reform an original whole; a process of removing "*fragmentation*" in data or knowledge to provide a clear understanding; applying techniques and processes that promote a *holistic* interconnected *al-*

pha state, favoring observational *Awareness* of continuity in all spiritual and physical systems; in *Systemology*, a "*Seeker*" achieving actualized "*Self-Honest Awareness*" is said to be in a basic state of *beta-defragmentation*, whereas *Alpha-defragmentation* is the rehabilitation of the *creative ability*, managing the *Spiritual Timeline* and the POV of *Self* as Alpha-Spirit (I-AM).

fragmentation : breaking into parts and scattering the pieces; the *fractioning* of wholeness or the *fracture* of a holistic interconnected *alpha* state, favoring observational *Awareness* of perceived connectivity between parts; *discontinuity*; separation of a totality into parts; in *Systemology*, a person outside of *Self-Honesty* is said to be operating from a *fragmented* state.

flow : movement across (or through) a channel (or conduit); a direction of active energetic motion, typically distinguished as either an *in-flow*, *out-flow* or *cross-flow*.

genetic-vehicle : a physical *Life*-form; the physical (*beta*) body that is animated/controlled by the (*Alpha*) *Spirit* using a continuous *Spiritual Lifeline* (ZU); a physical (*beta*) organic receptacle and catalyst for the (*Alpha*) *Self* to operate "causes" and experience "effects" within the *Physical Universe*.

harmful-act : a counter-survival mode of behavior or action (esp. that causes harm to one of more *Spheres of Existence*)—or—an overtly aggressive (hostile and/or destructive) action against an individual or any other *Sphere of Existence*; in *Utilitarian Systemology*—a short-sighted (serves fewest/lowest *Spheres of Existence*) intentional overtly harmful action to resolve a perceived problem; a revision of the rule for standard *Utilitarianism* for Systemology to distinguish actions which provide the least benefit to the least number of *Spheres of Existence*, or else the greatest harm to the greatest number of *Spheres of Existence*; in *moral philosophy*—an action which can be experienced by few and/or which one would not be willing to experience for themselves (*theft, slander, rape, &tc*); an iniquity or iniquitous act.

hold-back : withheld communications (esp. actions) such as "*Hold-Outs*"; intentional (or automatic) withdrawal (as opposed to reach); Self-restraint (which may eventually be enforced or automated); not reaching, acting or expressing, when one should be; an ability that is now restrained (on automatic) due to inability to withhold it on Self-determinism alone.

hold-outs : in photography, the numerous snapshots/pictures withheld from the final display or professional presentation of the event; withheld communications; in Utilitarian Systemology— energetic withdrawal and communication breaks with a "*terminal*" and its *Sphere of Existence* as a result of a "*Harmful-Act*"; unspoken or undiscovered (hidden, covert) actions that an individual withholds communications of, fearing punishment or endangerment of *Self-preservation* (*First Sphere*); the act of hiding (or keeping hidden) the truth of a "*Harmful-Act*"; a refusal to communicate with a *Pilot*; also "*Hold-Back.*"

holistic : the examination of interconnected systems as encompassing something greater than the *sum* of their "parts."

Human Condition : a standard default state of Human experience that is generally accepted to be the extent of its potential identity (*beingness*) —currently treated as *Homo Sapiens Sapiens,* but which is scheduled for replacement by *Homo Novus* (the "New Human").

imprint : to strongly impress, stamp, mark (or outline) onto a softer 'impressible' substance; to mark with pressure onto a surface; in *Systemology,* used to indicate permanent Reality impressions marked by frequencies, energies or interactions experienced during periods of emotional distress, pain, unconsciousness, loss, enforcement, or something antagonistic to physical (personal) survival, all of which are are stored with other reactive response-mechanisms at lower-levels of *Awareness* as opposed to the active memory database and proactive processing center of the Mind; an experiential "memory-set" that may later resurface—be triggered or stimulated artificially—as Reality, of which similar responses will be engaged automatically; holographic-like imagery "stamped" onto consciousness as composed of energetic *facets* tied to the "snap-shot" of an experience.

invalidate : decrease the level or degree or *agreement* as Reality.

pilot : a professional steersman responsible for healthy functional operation of a ship toward a specific destination; in *Systemology*, an intensive trained individual qualified to specially apply *Systemology Processing* to assist other *Seekers* on the *Pathway*.

point-of-view (POV) : a point to view from; an opinion or attitude as expressed from a specific identity-phase; a specific standpoint or vantage-point; a definitive manner of consideration specific to an individual phase or identity; a place or position affording a specific view or vantage; circumstances and programming of an individual that is conducive to a particular response, consideration or belief-set (paradigm); a position (consideration) or place (location) that provides a specific view or perspective (subjective) on experience (of the objective).

postulate : to put forward as truth; to suggest or assume an existence *to be*; to state or affirm the existence of particular conditions; to provide a basis of reasoning and belief; a basic theory accepted as fact; in *Systemology*, Alpha-Thought —the top-most decisions or considerations made by the Alpha-Spirit regarding the "*is-ness*" (what things "are") about energy-matter and space-time.

presence : a quality of some thing (*energy/matter*) being "present" in space-time; personal orientation of *Self* as an *Awareness* (*POV*) located in present space-time (environment) and communicating with extant energy-matter.

processing command line (PCL) or **command line** : a directed input; a specific command using highly selective language for *Systemology Processing*; a predetermined directive statement (cause) intended to focus concentrated attention (effect).

processing, systematic : the inner-workings or "through-put" result of systems; in *Systemology*, a method of applied spiritual technology used toward personal Self-Actualization; methods of selective directed attention, communicated language and associative imagery that increases personal control of the human condition.

realization : the clear perception of an understanding; a consideration or understanding on what is "actual"; to make "real" or give "reality" to so as to grant a property of "being-ness" or "being as it is"; the state or instance of coming to an *Awareness*; in *Systemology*, "gnosis" or true knowledge achieved during *systematic processing*; achievement of a new (or higher) cognition, true knowledge or perception of Self; a consideration of reality or assignment of meaning.

responsibility : the *ability* to *respond*; the extent of mobilizing *power* and *understanding* an individual maintains as *Awareness* to enact *change*; the proactive ability to *Self-direct* and make decisions independent of an outside authority.

Seeker : an individual on the *Pathway to Self-Honesty*; a practitioner of *Mardukite Systemology* or *Systemology Processing*, that is working toward *Spiritual Ascension*.

Self-actualization : bringing the full potential of the Human spirit into Reality; expressing full capabilities and creativeness of the *Alpha-Spirit*.

Self-determinism : the freedom to act, clear of external control or influence; the personal control of Will to direct intention.

Self-honesty : the basic or original *alpha* state of *being* and *knowing*; clear and present total *Awareness* of-and-as *Self*, in its most basic and true proactive expression of itself as *Spirit* or *I-AM*—free of artificial attachments, perceptive filters and other emotionally-reactive or mentally-conditioned programming imposed on the human condition by the systematized physical world; the ability to experience existence without judgment.

spiritual timeline : a continuous stream of moment-to-moment *Mental Images* (or a record of experiences) that defines the "past" of a spiritual being (or *Alpha-Spirit*) and which includes impressions (*imprints, &tc.*) from all life-incarnations and significant spiritual events the being has encountered; in Systemology, also "*backtrack.*"

Spheres of Existence : a series of *eight* concentric circles, rings or spheres (each larger than the former) that is overlaid onto the Standard Model of Beta-Existence to demonstrate the dynamic systems of existence extending out from the POV of Self (often as a "body") at the *First Sphere*; these are given in the basic eightfold systems as: *Self, Home/Family, Groups, Humanity, Life on Earth, Physical Universe, Spiritual Universe* and *Infinity-Divinity.*

Systemology : a modern tradition of applied religious philosophy and spiritual technology based on *Arcane Tablets* (in combination with *"general systemology"* and *"games theory"*) developed in the New Age underground by Joshua Free in 2011 as an advanced futurist extension of the *Mardukite Research Org.*; also known as *"Mardukite Systemology," "Metahuman Systemology"* and *"Spiritual Systemology."*

terminal (node) : a point, end, or mass, on a line; a connection point for closing an electric circuit, such as a post on a battery terminating at each end of its own systematic function; a point of connectivity with other points; in systems, a contact point of interaction; a point of interaction with other points.

turbulence : a quality or state of distortion or disturbance that creates irregularity of a flow or pattern; the quality or state of aberration on a line (such as ragged edges) or the emotional "turbulent feelings" attached to a particular flow or terminal node; a violent, haphazard or disharmonious commotion (such as in the ebb of gusts and lulls of wind action).

validation : a reinforcement of agreements or considerations as being "real."

viewpoint : see *"point-of-view" (POV)*.

willingness : the state of conscious Self-determined ability and interest (directed attention) to *Be*, *Do* or *Have*; a Self-determined consideration to reach, face up to (*confront*) or manage some "mass" or energy; the extent to which an individual considers themselves able to participate, act or communicate along some line, to put attention or intention on the line, or to produce (create) an effect.

ZU : the ancient Sumerian cuneiform sign for the archaic verb—*"to know," "knowingness"* or *"awareness"*; in *Mardukite Zuism and Systemology*, the active energy/matter of the "Spiritual Universe" (AN) experienced as a *Lifeforce* or *consciousness* that imbues living forms extant in the "Physical Universe" (KI); *"Spiritual Life Energy"*; energy demonstrated by the WILL of an actualized *Alpha-Spirit* in the "Spiritual Universe" (AN), which impinges its *Awareness* into the Physical Universe (KI), animating/controlling *Life* for its experience of *beta-existence* along an individual Alpha-Spirit's personal *Identity-continuum*, called a *ZU-line*.

Zu-**Line** : a theoretical construct in *Mardukite*

Zuism and Systemology demonstrating *Spiritual Life Energy* (*ZU*) as a personal individual "continuum" of Awareness interacting with all Spheres of Existence on the Standard Model of Systemology; a spectrum of potential variations and interactions of a monistic continuum or singular *Spiritual Life Energy* demonstrated on the Standard Model; an energetic channel of potential POV and "locations" of Beingness, demonstrated in early Systemology materials as an individual Alpha-Spirit's personal *Identity- continuum*, potentially connecting *Awareness* of *Self* with "*Infinity*" simultaneous with all points considered in existence; a symbolic demonstration of the "*Life-line*" on which *Awareness (ZU)* extends from the direction of the "Spiritual Universe" (AN) in its true original *alpha state* through an entire possible range of activity resulting in its *beta state* and control of a *genetic-entity* occupying the *Physical Universe (KI)*.

Zu-Vision : the true and basic (*Alpha*) Point-of-View (perspective, POV) maintained by *Self* as *Alpha-Spirit* outside boundaries or considerations of the *Human Condition* and *exterior* to beta-existence reality agreements with the Physical Universe; a POV of Self *as* "a unit of Spiritual Awareness" that exists independent of a "body" and entrapment in a *Human Condition*; "spirit vision" in its truest sense.

88

Fundamentals of Systemology
in six
Basic Course Lesson Booklets

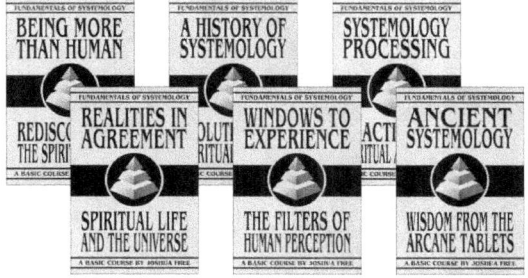

Also
available
as a
six-in-one
hardcover
edition!

THE SYSTEMOL

Seekers and students of the *Basic Course* and *Professional Course* will also be interested in the *Advanced Series* of the *Systemology Core*. These volumes are a complete chronological record of the Mardukite New Thought developments from the Systemology Society, published in 2019 through 2023.

The *Systemology Core* begins with the first professional publication released when the *Mardukite Systemology Society* emerged from the underground in 2019, with: *"The Tablets of Destiny Revelation."*

OGY PATHWAY

The Tablets of Destiny Revelation:
*How Long-Lost Anunnaki Wisdom
Can Change the Fate of Humanity*

Crystal Clear: *Handbook for Seekers*

Metahuman Destinations (*2 volumes*)

Imaginomicon:
Approaching Gateways to Higher Universes

Way of the Wizard: *Utilitarian Systemology*

Systemology-180: *Fast-Track to Ascension*

Systemology Backtrack:
Reclaiming Spiritual Power & Past-Life Memory

PUBLISHED BY THE **JOSHUA FREE** IMPRINT REPRESENTING

The Mardukite Academy of Systemology

THE JOSHUA FREE IMPRINT
JFI PUBLICATIONS

MARDUKITE
ZUISM

mardukite.com

www.ingramcontent.com/pod-product-compliance
Lightning Source LLC
Chambersburg PA
CBHW071213120626
46546CB00006B/2539